HOW TO CREATE A

DIGITAL FORT KNOX

BACKING UP YOUR DIGITAL LIFE

DIY Step By Step Easy and Affordable Unraid Server Backup Solution

By Joseph William Cristina

Trademarks

All terms mentioned in this book that are known to be trademarks or service marks have been appropriately capitalized. The author and publisher cannot attest to the accuracy of this information. Use of a term in the book should not be regarded as affecting the validity of any trademark or service mark.

Unraid® "Unraid" mentioned herein, is a registered trademark of Lime Technology, Inc.

Warning and Disclaimer

This book is designed to provide information about Unraid®. Every effort has been made to make this book as complete and as accurate as possible, but no warranty of fitness is implied.

The information is provided on an as-is basis. The authors and publisher shall have neither liability nor responsibility to any person or entity with respect to any loss or damages arising from the information contained in this book.

The thoughts, opinions, and documented experiences found within this publication are solely those of the author and are in no way those of any party referenced herein.

Moreover, the author is in no way associated with Lime Technology, Inc., the makers of Unraid® software, and is simply a pro user that wishes to share his experiences with the reader.

This book is dedicated to my family for their support and understanding of me not being present during the countless hours of work that went into its creation.

To my wife and kids for always believing in me.

What? You're writing another book?
We thought you were working on a new invention!

To my parents for providing me with a strong work ethic. Immigrating into this country with no money and not speaking a word of English to owning a construction company and running the medical laboratory in one of the largest hospitals in South Florida.

Finally, a special thank you to Homero A. Gonzalez for his friendship and proofreading expertise.

With dedication and hard work, dreams are attainable. Drive, focus, and perseverance levels the playing field no matter how humble our beginnings.

TABLE OF CONTENTS

TABLE OF CONTENTS

TABLE OF CONTENTS

TABLE OF CONTENTS

TABLE OF CONTENTS

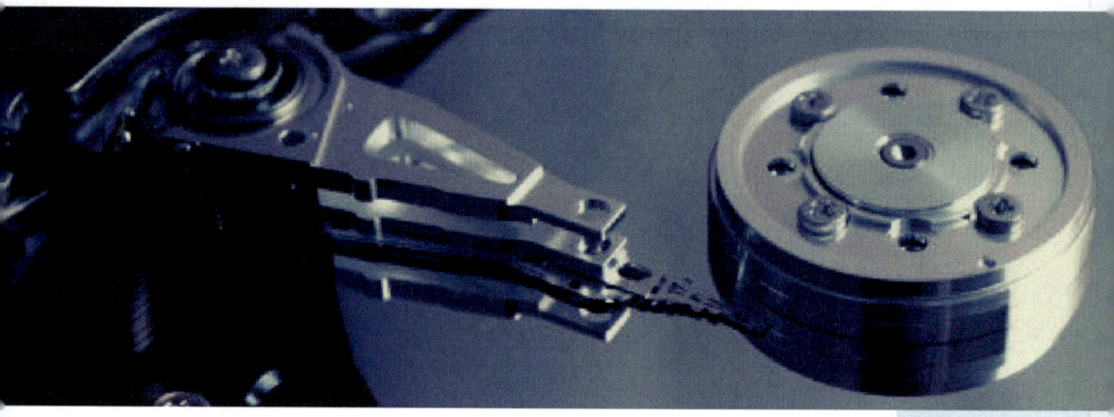

In today's digital world we produce vast amounts of data; photos, videos, music, documents, and more. Our risk of catastrophic data loss has also vastly increased. I hope you're already aware of the ***3-2-1 backup rule*** but if you're not, this time-honored backup strategy states that you should have 3 copies of your data at all times. A primary copy, "live data" you're working on (ie. on an SSD), a second copy, "archival data" on a separate computer or backup appliance using an alternative media type (hard drive, flash, tape, etc.), and finally a third copy stored off-site for disaster recovery "cold storage data".

This book covers the archival data backup portion of the 3-2-1 rule by providing a step-by-step easy, and affordable method of creating a safe and secure local data backup solution, your very own ***Digital Fort Knox***, called an **Unraid Server**.

3-2-1

backup strategy

"3 copies of data, stored on 2 different types of storage media, and one copy should be kept offsite"

Most of us have heard or even use "**THE CLOUD**", cloud storage, cloud backups, cloud, cloud, cloud, cloud, cloud... The question we must ask ourselves is simply what happens when stormy weather comes and the cloud opens up and our data is lost forever? It is not unheard of for large corporations to lose client cloud-stored data due to a "glitch". The bottom line is, cloud storage is not as secure as many believe it to be and most company's terms of service provide them legal protection if data is lost.

- Your cloud services provider may discontinue its service
- Your cloud services provider may experience a hardware crash
- Your cloud services provider may experience a software glitch
- Your cloud services provider may get hacked or sustain a ransomware attack
- You or your employees may delete critical data by accident

For these reasons and many more, the critical data that you keep in the cloud could be lost forever with absolutely no possibility of retrieval.

We must understand that using "THE CLOUD" is fine for non-critical data or even as a secondary or tertiary means of offsite backup but never as a primary storage location.

This is where a local archival backup is one of the most important safeguards to protect valuable personal and client data. Not only does it provide peace of mind that your data is backed up redundantly but also that it's close at hand for immediate access if necessary.

"
It's imperative
to safeguard
your digital life!

Being a professional photographer, videographer, artist, and content creator for over 20 years losing personal or client project data has always been a point of stress in my life. This worry made me constantly make backups of my work on countless external hard drives and then back up those backups for added security. Over time, photos went from 10 megapixels to over 100 and video from 720p, 1080p, 4K, and now even 8K.

Subsequently, file sizes became larger and larger and so did my library of external backup hard drives. The problem was 'search and rescue'. You see, even though I knew I had all my projects and personal files backed up and those backups were also backed up the problem was if I needed to locate a specific file it would take hours to sort through the dozens upon dozens, literally piles, of hard drives to find what I or a client needed.

I tried sorting the drives by year then by month and even by project but it simply was impractical and added even more stress to my life.

Eventually, I stumbled upon a backup solution called a RAID Server where I could store all of the data from the many dozens of hard drives onto one centralized location (Server) and access said data locally or even remotely if need be from anywhere on the planet with an internet connection.

This sounded too good to be true and it kinda was. RAID Servers, while redundantly backing up data across multiple hard drives are great for speed and protection, while a positive, can quickly turn into a negative if multiple hard drives were to fail at the same time. As luck would have it (sarcasm), Murphy's Law was right, “If anything can go wrong, it will”.

For example, using a RAID 5 setup if (1) one hard drive was to fail simply replace the (1) one bad drive with a new one, and the system would automatically rebuild the RAID array allowing for zero downtime and zero data loss.

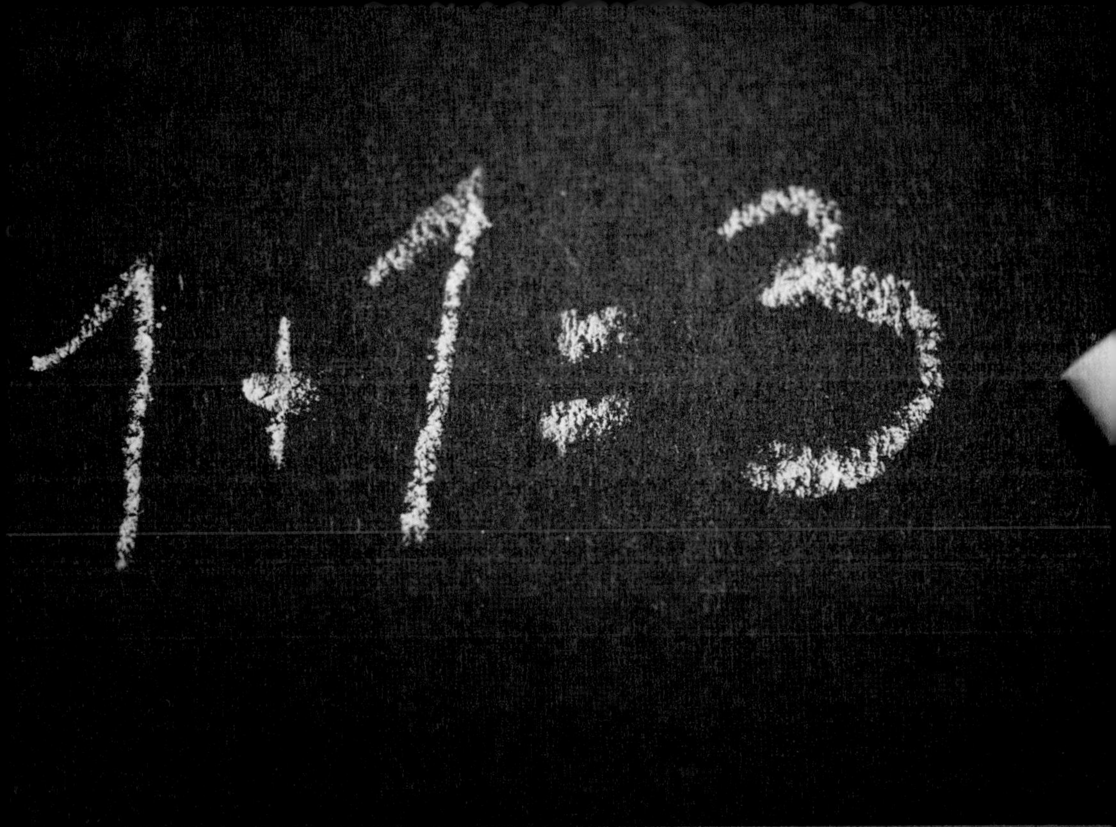

If anything can go wrong, it will

- Murphy's Law

If (2) two of the (5) five drives were to fail, which happened to me, two days apart, then not only would you no longer be able to access your data on the (2) two bad drives, but all data on all (5) five drives would be permanently lost. Once again, if 2 out of the 5 drives fail, everything is lost!

That's right, all of your data would be gone!

As you can imagine this simply didn't work for me so I continued doing my multiple redundant back-ups on more and even more external drives until finally, I found a solution that was perfect for all my archival backup needs.

It's called an Unraid Server.

While it's very similar to a proper RAID Server it has a few pros and cons and for me, the pros far outweigh the cons.

Unlike a conventional RAID Server, the mere fact that I didn't have to use all of the same size hard drives in the array dramatically lowered the initial cost of the Unraid Server. Being able to combine any of the countless hard drives that I already had 1TB, 2TB, 5TB, 8TB, etc. instead of being forced to purchase all new hard drives was a major pro for me.

Although the read/write speeds were a bit slower than a conventional RAID Server, for archival backup this was a non-issue, and most of all, if multiple drives were to fail in an Unraid Server setup only the data on the broken drives would be lost while the data on the remaining working drives would still be fully accessible.

I was sold and my first Unraid Server called Harley was constructed over a weekend using a ten-year-old PC and extra components I unearthed from my garage.

Harley has been in service 24/7 for just over a year without a single problem and all of those countless external hard drives are a thing of the past. My stress level has gone from an 11 on a scale from 0 to 10 down to a 3.

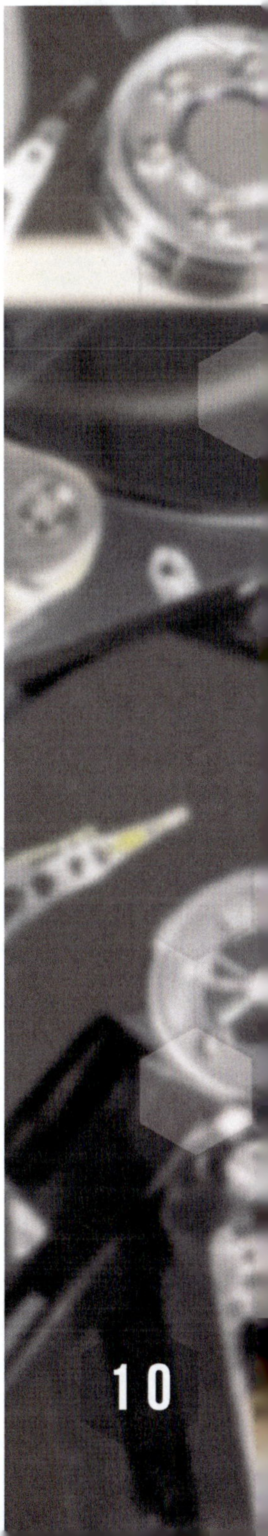

"All those countless external hard drives are a thing of the past"

You may ask why my stress level was still at a three and not zero. Well, every good backup requires 3 copies and one must be off-site so while I have 100% peace of mind locally, I still must back up important data to another location following the 3-2-1 backup rule to feel fully secure.

In this book, I'll show you the basics of setting up and configuration an Unraid Server, using new or even old parts you may have available. I'm confident, using this server to organize and safeguard your valuable personal and client data will greatly reduce your digital life stress as it has mine.

Who needs to locally backup their digital life

The short answer is everyone! For the most part today, we are all content creators producing at times gigabytes or even terabytes of documents, photos, videos, and audio on an ongoing basis. If these memories or projects are not securely archived they will certainly be lost to the sands of digital time.

"Everyone should have a local backup"

Today we produce gigabytes or even terabytes of documents, photos, videos, and audio on an ongoing basis.

What is a local archival backup?

A local archival backup is a redundant copy of your working “live data" Photos, videos, audio, or any other digital documents. Think of this local backup server as the Digital Fort Knox for your digital life. This is where your data is redundantly stored and can be easily accessed and searched locally or even remotely if so desired.

Where to store local archival backups?

Hence the name, local, these archival backups should remain in reach. In case of data loss, you can access your Digital Fort Knox immediately.

When and how often should you backup?

In most cases, backups should be conducted constantly in the background without you having to intercede.

Why is it important to have a local backup instead of a cloud backup?

Security, accessibility, and speed of restoration. You are not dependent on a third party to store and secure your data. If God forbid, you somehow lose any of your critical data, and connectivity is lost (internet is down), with a local backup, you're 100% covered while data stored in the cloud would be inaccessible for the duration of the outage.

What happens when the internet goes down?

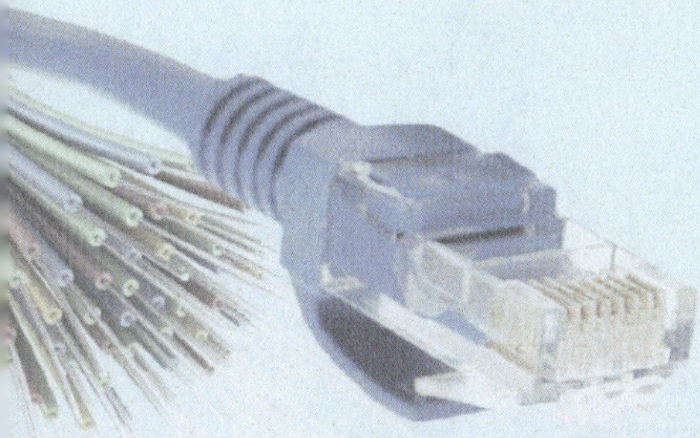

NO CONNECTION = NO DATA

Unable To Connect To The Internet

Why should I use Unraid instead of RAID?

Confidence is begotten by understanding the unit and not putting your trust in the man behind the curtain!

Unlike the Unraid Server, some turn-key RAID Backup solutions (appliances) have been hit by ransomware and other data comprising attacks due to back doors and various security issues.

Unraid provides the ability to start small and add capacity as needed with fewer restrictions over a standard RAID Server Setup while providing the exact amount of security the user requires.

Unraid allows you to use any size drive in the array as long as it's equal to or less than the size of the parity drive. Mixing and matching allow you to use ANY of your older hard drives, regardless of size or speed, instead of having to buy all new for the server.

If a multi-drive failure were to occur with most Off-The-Shelf RAID servers running a proprietary RAID5 setup, everything, yes everything, would be permanently lost!

However, with Unraid Server, only the data on the drives that failed would be lost. All data on the unaffected drives would be fully secure and accessible.

Nothing is perfect, Unraid does have one drawback and that is speed. Unraid is an archival backup solution and does not employ data striping to increase read and write speeds. That being said, I've edited UHD Video over a Gigabit LAN on this Unraid Server during testing with absolutely no issues. Your miles may vary!

Well, if you made it this far, congratulations! I think you're ready to put together your own Unraid Server, configure it, and start backing up your digital life.

If not, I hate to see you go but you can always come back when you're ready to take this journey with me.

https://jcristina.com/books

Grab a cup of tea, coffee, or maybe something a bit harder, and let's get started!

https://jcristina.com/books

BUILDING AND CONFIGURING A BASIC UNRAID SERVER

Buy New or Build Used

Option 1

Buy a New PC tower computer ready to go

> If this is more your speed than congratulations you've just reduced your build time by half but you'll notice your wallet has been equally reduced. :) You can jump straight over to **Setup & Configuration**. *See Table Of Contents*

Option 2

Go to your garage and pull out some old parts.

> Glad you're here! I'm certain the people that chose Option 1 are already gone so between you and me, I like you much better! :) We frugal nerds need to stick together so...
> Let's jump right in!

Building Your Server

As a means of demonstrating that new expensive equipment is in most cases not necessary, I provide a list of older parts and ***why*** they were selected to build this Unraid server.

> Why would I take the time to provide you with the reason?

It's quite simple, in a one-word answer, evergreen. You see, due to location, time, and even budget, you would most likely not be able to obtain every part that I'm using today and certainly if you were building this unit in the distant future.

That all being said, by providing you with the knowledge and understanding of part selection this book will continue to be an asset for many years to come. I've deliberately used older components to show that shiny new "expensive" parts are not required to build a reliable, safe, and secure Unraid Server. Save your money but if you find that it's burning a hole in your pocket consider buying me a hot cup of tea.

The authors' tip jar PayPal account

jctipjar@gmail.com

"
Time is the most valuable thing a man can spend.
- Theophrastus
"

My Parts List

Full-Size Computer Tower Case

Cooler Master Case

Why

While I could have used a mid-sized tower case I went with a full-sized unit. This provides more internal space for hard drives and the added flexibility of using a hot-swappable drive bay. These drive bays while not required makes for drive extraction and replacing a breeze. Also, the larger size provides better airflow while physically allowing for more fans to be installed. Simply put, good airflow keeps temperatures down and extends the life of your hardware.

"SIZE Matters"

MotherBoard

ABIT IX37 Intel(R) Core(TM)2 Quad CPU Q6600 @ 2.40GHz with 6 7pin SATA-300 Serial ATA Connectors and Cables

That's right! c.2008 - Over decade old!

Why

In this case, it's all about the bare necessities. ATX form factor to drop right into a Mini, Mid, or Full Tower size case and uses an LGA775 Socket Pentium CPU (*I had a few laying around*)

Note

When you purchase a motherboard, make sure it's compatible with the CPU you want to use or buy a used or new motherboard/CPU combo to be safe. For this build, processing power is not very important to an UnRaid Server providing general archival functionality. But, if you were building this unit to be a PLEX Media Server used to stream all of your audio, photos, and even movies/tv-shows a more powerful motherboard/CPU combo is recommended. * Plex configuration is for a future advanced book * Also, I would suggest a motherboard that can support at least six hard drives without the need to purchase a SATA add-on controller board.

Memory

4 Memory Sticks [PC2-6400U 2GB Modules]

Why

This motherboard only holds 8GB of memory so, I installed 4-2GB modules to max it out. For your system, you might be able to install 8GB, 16GB, 32GB, 64GB, 128GB, or even more. An Unraid Server only requires 2GB of RAM to function but installing 8GB or even more will help future proof your setup.

Note

Unraid Current Minimum Requirements (1)

- General Services (FTP, Databases, VoIP, etc.): 2GB of RAM (although 4GB is recommended), 1 CPU Core
- Content Download and Extraction (SABnzbd, NZBget, etc.): 4GB of RAM, 2 CPU cores
- Media Servers (Plex, Logitech, Universal, etc.): 4GB of RAM, Intel i5/i7/e3 processor
- Virtual Servers (Windows, Arch, etc.): 256MB - 1GB, 1-2 CPU cores
- Virtual Desktops (Windows, Ubuntu, etc.): 512MB - 8GB, 2-4 CPU cores
- Hybrid VMs (GPU assignment, gaming, etc.): 1GB - 12GB, 2-6 CPU cores

"The more
the merrier"

GPU (Graphics Processing Unit)

AMD RV630 PRO [Radeon HD 2600 PRO]

Why

While a GPU (Graphics Processing Unit) is not needed for day-to-day use as you can access your server from any computer on your local network via its IP address. A GPU, in my opinion, makes configuration a bit easier.

Note

Like all other parts, I recommend using name-brand as it will more likely be compatible with Unraid and Linux Distro used by Lime Technology. An Unraid Server more times than not a set-it and forget-it appliance. It does its work in the background without you having to do anything besides monitor if you need to swap out a drive that's failing and update or patch applications or the OS. Some of my servers have uptimes (duration of time the unit has been in operation without reboot) for over 750 days. That's Right! More than two years without restarting the server.

Power Supply

Cooler Master 750W ATX 12V v.2.2

Overkill but I had it laying around!

Why

In general, a barebones system using a standard video card will use approximately 200w of power and each hard drive around 30w. For a six hard-drive setup, we can estimate usage of (30w * 6)+200w= 380w. I recommend a supply with at least 100w headroom for spikes and overall unit longevity. A power system with 500-550 watts would work perfectly for this system.

Note

As the cost of SSD (Solid State Drives) comes down, it will become more affordable to use more of these drives in our server builds. SSD drives not only lower power consumption but also heat and noise production.

Also, the power supply needs to have the same connectors as required by the motherboard. i.e. an ATX motherboard requires an ATX power connector.

Hard Drives

5 Seagate IRONWOLF NAS
1 Samsung 860 EVO 250GB SSD (Solid State Drive)

Why

You will find many hard drive makers on the market from Seagate, Western Digital, IBM, and countless others. The main thing you want to take into account is the intended use of the drive. Even though you'll be tempted by the price, you should stay away from shucked drives that were pulled out of cheap store-bought backup units or no-name brands. In general, these are cheap for a reason! Stay away from general use drives as they are not made for server workloads. I would suggest spending the money on quality NAS or Enterprise Class drives from the beginning even if this means you can only afford 3 drives now. Unlike store-bought RAID backup servers that the quality of the drives is unknown, with your server you are able to purchase the best drives (no matter size or speed) and add them into the mix at any time with very little effort.

The Samsung 860 EVO is a cache drive. A pit stop for your data to wait to be shuttled over to the backup hard drives for archival storage. You can use a hard drive for this purpose, but I suggest an SSD as this will speed up your data transfer rates considerably. Solid-state drives SSD have faster transfer rates and some argue are more reliable with no mechanical parts.

Choose the right tool for the job

PRO TIP

Purchasing drives from different manufacturers or at least from different vendors assures you don't receive units from the same lot. This will reduce the possibility of multiple drives failing at the same time!

Optional Hard Drive Hot Swap Bay

Why

While you can certainly skip this unit altogether and mount your drives in the drive bays provided within your case, for me, a server is not complete without hot-swappable drive bays providing the ability to pull hard drives in and out without having to turn off the system. When the time comes when a failing hard drive needs to be replaced you'll be thankful that you spent a couple of extra bucks on this add-on.

Keyboard & Mouse

Why

While you can set up, configure, and maintain the Unraid Server through the local network, it is much easier to use a keyboard & mouse during installation.

Note

Stick with a hardwired keyboard and mouse. There's no reason to worry about driver issues. KISS principle! (Keep It Simple Stupid)

PARTS CHECKLIST

- [ ] Case + Extra Fans + Power Supply
- [ ] Hot-Swappable Drive Bay *(Optional)*
- [ ] Mother Board + CPU
- [ ] Memory
- [ ] Data Drives
- [ ] Parity Drive(s)
- [ ] Cache Drive(s)
- [ ] Graphics Card *(Onboard Is Fine)*
- [ ] USB Pen Drive
- [ ] Keyboard & Mouse
- [ ] UPS Battery Backup
- [ ] Additional Parts
- [ ] Additional Parts
- [ ] Additional Parts

Setup & Configuration

What we need for initial Unraid Server installation

Name Brand USB 2.0 Stick 8GB to 32GB in size

- **Do not buy junk!** Here's where your operating system will be stored
- SanDisk, PNY, Samsung, Patriot, Kingston are just a few great choices
- 2.0 is fast enough and is generally more compatible
- Must have a GUID so that it can be made bootable and registered
- A small low-profile form factor is perfect as it will remain installed on the back of the PC or on the motherboard itself.

Download Unraid Software

From the following URL download the PC or MAC version of Unraid from Lime Technology's

https://unraid.net/download

That which we call a rose by any other name would smell as sweet

- William Shakespeare

Sorry William, not in this case. Buy name brand and you'll thank me later!

UNRAID PRODUCT PRICING COMMUNITY BLOG APPS DOCS

Download Unraid Server OS

Download and install the software to your server. Once the software is installed, you can either purchase the Registration Key of your choice or request a Trial Key. Registration requires a valid USB Flash GUID. See our Getting Started Guide for details on setting up Unraid Server OS.

Don't worry... We will discuss picking the right License Key for your use case later.

Formating USB / Installing OS

Run the **USB Creator** software file you've down downloaded on your current computer.

Select Stable

For this build, we will be using the **STABLE** version of the Unraid Server.

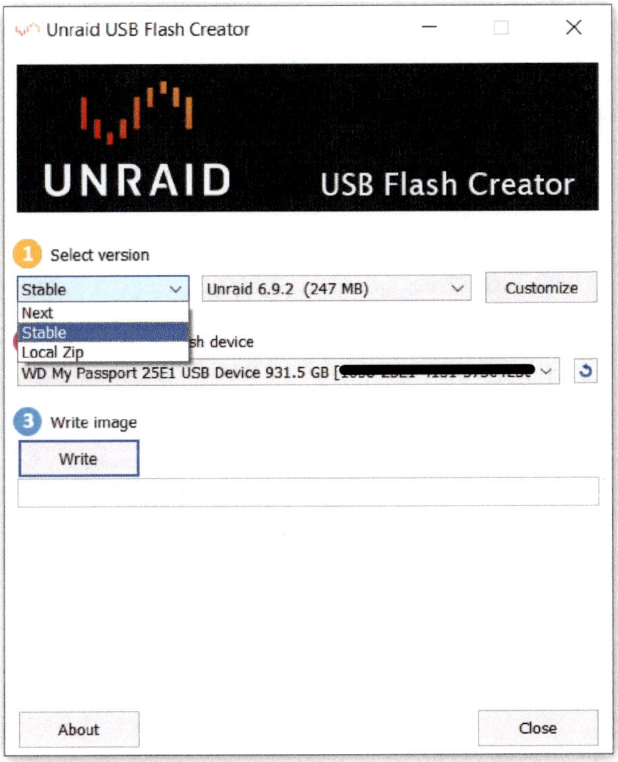

Select The Latest Version

The latest version may have changed since the time of publication. That's OK. Select the most recent stable version unless you have a good reason for selecting an old version.

Select USB Drive

It's **<u>CRITICAL</u>** that you check, re-check and check again that you've selected the correct USB drive! This drive will be formatted and **<u>ALL</u>** data will be permanently lost. Maybe I should repeat this!

Check, re-check, and check again that you've selected the correct USB Drive used!

Click On Customize

Leave the **Network Mode** setting to **DHCP** unless you are a computer GOD and feel the need to have a Static IP address for your server. **DHCP** will allow the server to automatically obtain any available IP address on your network without your intervention.

Click Server Name

Select a name you would like to call your server
Mine is called **Harley**... Don't judge!
I'm a fan of Harley Quinn if you didn't know!

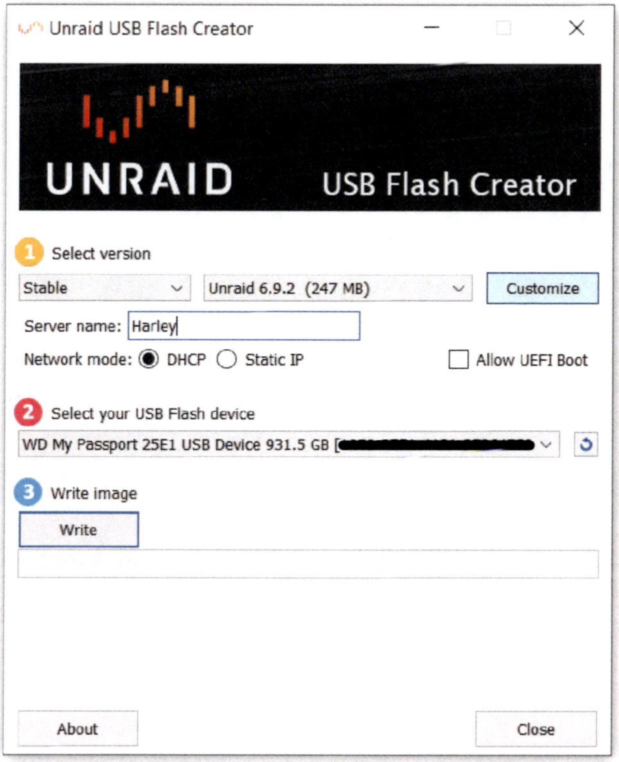

Check Allow UEFI Boot

If you have a motherboard that allows UEFI booting, set it to ALLOW so Unraid can boot directly from the USB Drive we are creating. The 10-year-old motherboard I pulled out of the garage does, so you should be OK.

Click on Write

You will be asked if you would like to ease everything on the stick and write the software select **Erase and Write**. The USB stick will be formatted, Unraid software downloaded and installed.

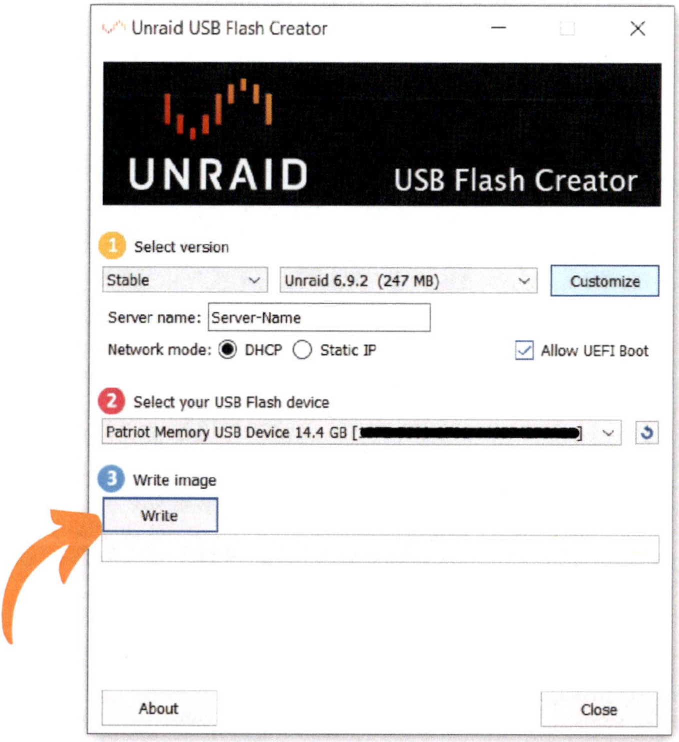

Boot For The First Time

Install the USB

Place the stick into your new server

Boot Into BIOS Setting *F12, F2, ESC, TAB, DEL, etc.*

To enter the BIOS varies from machine to machine check your motherboard manual for the method.

BIOS Menu

In the BIOS Menu go to the **Boot Section**

*Set the boot mode to **UEFI** if you have a **UEFI** motherboard*

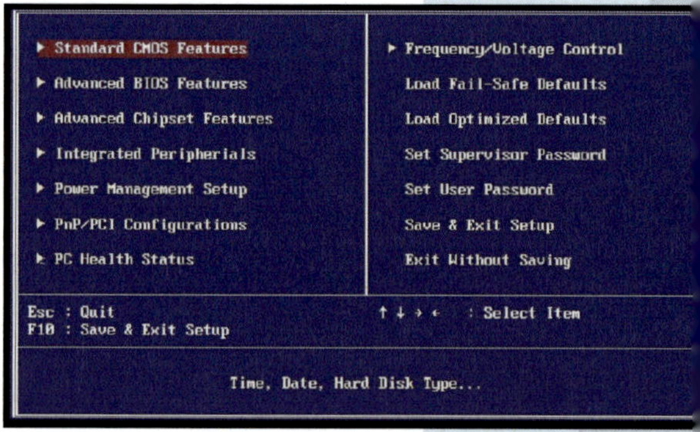

Change Boot Order

Change the boot order so that the USB Key is the first drive to boot

Save, Exit, and Reboot

It's time to boot into your brand new Unraid Server from the USB Stick you just created

Once booted, you'll see an IP address for your Unraid Server. You can use this or the server name from your browser to access the Unraid dashboard. For example

unRAID Server OS version: 6.9.2
IPv4 address: 192.168.1.78
IPv6 address: not set

"
You did it!
"
I knew you had it in you...
Congratulations

Configuring OS

Select the first option

Unraid OS ←
Unraid OS GUI Mode
Unraid OS Safe Mode (no plugins, no GUI)
Unraid OS GUI Safe Mode (no plugins)
Memtest86+

Once the Unraid server OS fully boots up and is connected to your local network, you can set it aside. We will complete the configuration process using a web browser interface on any computer connected to the same network.

Unraid Dashboard

Accessing your Unraid Server Dashboard

2 ways of accessing the Unraid Server Dashboard

- Type the IP address provided at installation into your web browser (example: http://**192.168.1.78**)
- Type the server name into your browser URL (example: http://**Harley**)

You should now see your Unraid DASHBOARD and will automatically get redirected to the Unraid key registration page.

Picking The Right License

At this point, you will need to decide which product key license you would like to purchase. A 30-day free trial may be available for a key based on the maximum number of drives you wish to use in your Unraid configuration.

Don't worry, you can always upgrade in the future. For this build, the 6 attached storage device license key will be perfect, and as of today, the cost is **$59/US**.

- **Basic - Up to 6 attached storage devices**
- **Plus - Up to 12 attached storage devices**
- **Pro - Unlimited attached storage devices**

Consult Lime Technology, Inc.'s. website for current pricing.

6 Drive Setup (*attached storage devices*) **Examples**

Cache drives are not included in the calculation. Meaning, a 6 attached storage device key will allow for 6 data storage drives and one or two cache drives within the Unraid Server.

As of writing this text, the largest Enterprise/NAS SATA drive is 18TB and we will be using it as a basis for our calculations.

Before going any further, let me explain the purpose of the various drives in our Unraid server.

Understanding Drive Types

Cache Drive

This drive holds the data when entering the Unraid server and as it fills up or at set intervals will unload its content onto a data storage drive. One or Two drives can be used for this task. I suggest using SSD drive(s) as it will increase transfer speeds. For added protection, you can use two cache drives that will mirror each other in case of failure before the cached data unloads to a data drives.

Parity Drive

The Parity drive is what keeps your data safe. Without having to write another book about this subject let's just say if you have one parity drive in the server you could have a single drive fail and not lose any data. With a two-drive parity setup, you would be able to have two drives fail without experiencing any data loss. I use one parity drive as it would be very rare that two out of five drives would fail on the same day or week providing ample time to replace the faulty drive. Furthermore, unlike a standard RAID server, if two drives were to go bad before being replaced, only the data on those two drives would be lost while all data on the good drives would be fully secure and accessible. For added protection, of course, you can set up two parity drives instead of one.

Backup Drive

These drives are the grunts. They are the workers that securely store all of your critical data for safekeeping and provide instant access 24/7 and 365 days a year.

Sample 6 Drive Setup

6 Drive Setup 1 Parity Drive Setup

5 - 18TB Data Storage = **90TB** of Usable Storage

6 Drive Setup 2 Parity Drive Setup

4 - 18TB Data Storage Drives = **72TB** of Usable Storage

12 Drive Setup would provide up to **2X** for both of the above setups. **180TB / 144TB** respectively.

Bear in mind, you **do not** need to use 18TB drives. You could mix and match 2TB, 10TB, and say 18TB drives. That's one of the great features of the Unraid server.

Note

The largest drive you can use in your Unraid server can not exceed the size of the parity drive(s). In simple terms, if you had a 12TB parity drive(s) in your Unraid server, the largest drive you could use as a data storage drive would be equal to or less than 12TB.

Assigning Hard Drives

You'll be prompted to assign drives attached to your system to different functions, **parity, data, and cache** drives for your setup.

From the dropdown menu, select the drives you wish to use for **Parity** and **Data Storage**.

Now select the SSD (Solid State Drive) you want to use as a **Cache Drive**.

> You can select two drives as cache drives. If you do, Unraid will automatically RAID1 (mirror) the two drives so that even while your data is waiting for offloading to the Data Storage drives, it'll remain protected.

Starting The Array

Go to the **MAIN** tab

Press the **START** button under **Array Operation**.

The system will begin doing a parity check which will test the drives and data on the drives for errors. This process is extremely slow and can take hours to even days to complete depending on the number of drives and their size.

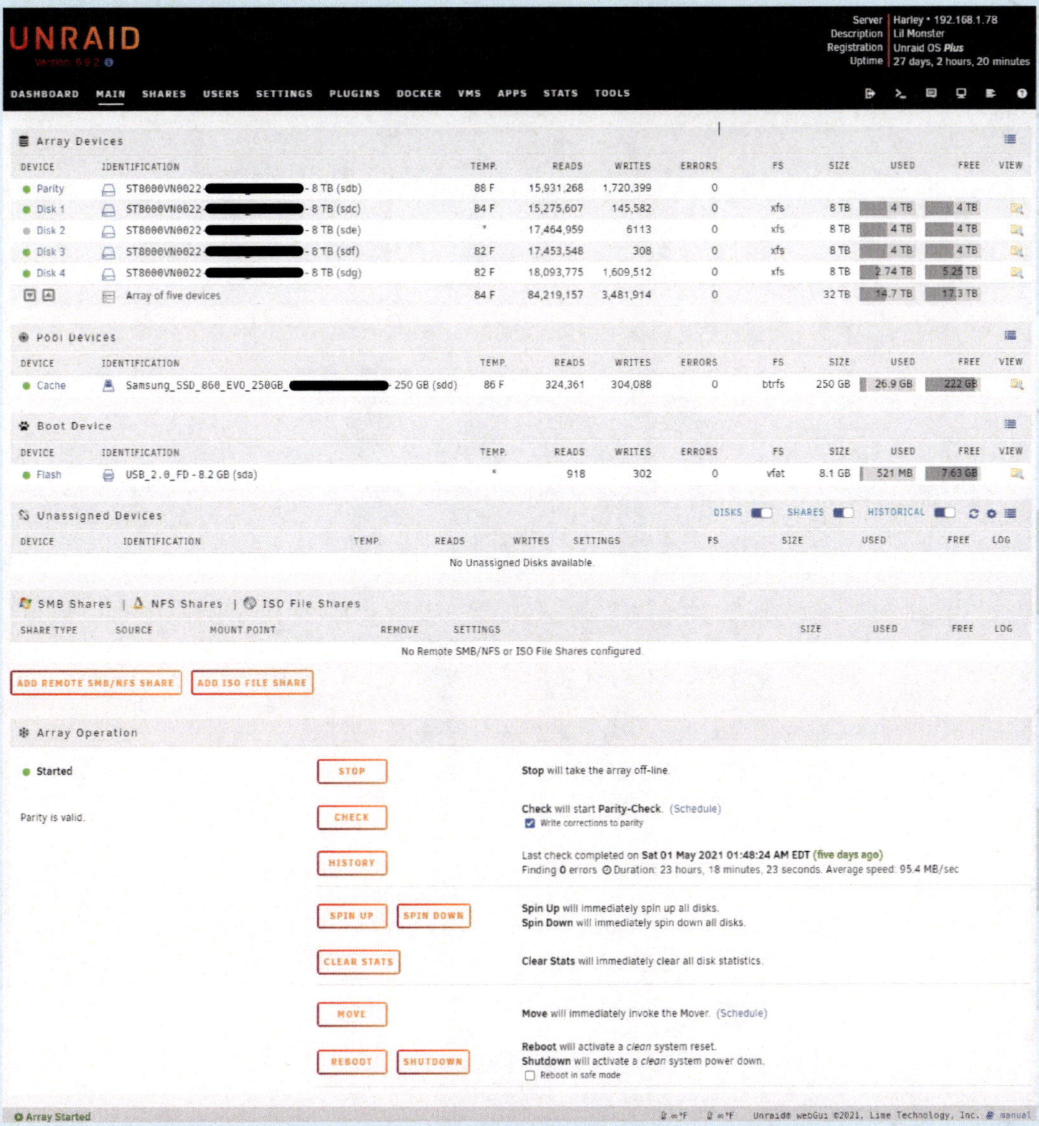

UNRAID
Server Harley • 192.168.1.78
Description Lil Monster
Registration Unraid OS Plus
Uptime 27 days, 2 hours, 20 minutes
DASHBOARD MAIN SHARES USERS SETTINGS PLUGINS DOCKER VMS APPS STATS TOOLS
Array Devices
DEVICE IDENTIFICATION TEMP. READS WRITES ERRORS FS SIZE USED FREE VIEW
Parity ST8000VN0022-[redacted]- 8 TB (sdb) 88 F 15,931,268 1,720,399 0
Disk 1 ST8000VN0022-[redacted]- 8 TB (sdc) 84 F 15,275,607 145,582 0 xfs 8 TB 4 TB 4 TB
Disk 2 ST8000VN0022-[redacted]- 8 TB (sde) * 17,464,959 6113 0 xfs 8 TB 4 TB 4 TB
Disk 3 ST8000VN0022-[redacted]- 8 TB (sdf) 82 F 17,453,548 308 0 xfs 8 TB 4 TB 4 TB
Disk 4 ST8000VN0022-[redacted]- 8 TB (sdg) 82 F 18,093,775 1,609,512 0 xfs 8 TB 2.74 TB 5.25 TB
Array of five devices 84 F 84,219,157 3,481,914 0 32 TB 14.7 TB 17.3 TB
Pool Devices
DEVICE IDENTIFICATION TEMP. READS WRITES ERRORS FS SIZE USED FREE VIEW
Cache Samsung_SSD_860_EVO_250GB_[redacted]- 250 GB (sdd) 86 F 324,361 304,088 0 btrfs 250 GB 26.9 GB 222 GB
Boot Device
DEVICE IDENTIFICATION TEMP. READS WRITES ERRORS FS SIZE USED FREE VIEW
Flash USB_2.0_FD - 8.2 GB (sda) * 918 302 0 vfat 8.1 GB 521 MB 7.63 GB
Unassigned Devices
DISKS SHARES HISTORICAL
DEVICE IDENTIFICATION TEMP. READS WRITES SETTINGS FS SIZE USED FREE LOG
No Unassigned Disks available.
SMB Shares | NFS Shares | ISO File Shares
SHARE TYPE SOURCE MOUNT POINT REMOVE SETTINGS SIZE USED FREE LOG
No Remote SMB/NFS or ISO File Shares configured.
ADD REMOTE SMB/NFS SHARE
ADD ISO FILE SHARE
Array Operation
Started
STOP
Stop will take the array off-line.
Parity is valid.
CHECK
Check will start Parity-Check. (Schedule)
Write corrections to parity
HISTORY
Last check completed on Sat 01 May 2021 01:48:24 AM EDT (five days ago)
Finding 0 errors Duration: 23 hours, 18 minutes, 23 seconds. Average speed: 95.4 MB/sec
SPIN UP
SPIN DOWN
Spin Up will immediately spin up all disks.
Spin Down will immediately spin down all disks.
CLEAR STATS
Clear Stats will immediately clear all disk statistics.
MOVE
Move will immediately invoke the Mover. (Schedule)
REBOOT
SHUTDOWN
Reboot will activate a clean system reset.
Shutdown will activate a clean system power down.
Reboot in safe mode
Array Started
Unraid® webGui ©2021, Lime Technology, Inc. manual

YOU
GOT
THIS

Format Drives

Under the **Start Button**, you will find a **Format Button**.

First click the radial button **[*] Yes**, I want to do this!

(you understand all data will be lost from the drives during formatting)

Protecting Your ROOT Account

Admin Account

Go to the **USER Tab**

Click on the **ROOT** User account

It is important to change your Unraid Server ROOT account password. This will help prevent people accessing your Network/WIFI from obtaining full administrative access to your server, as that could be devastating!

Click on **Password** and enter a new password you will not forget.

> *I suggest a **minimum** 8 character password, with 2 uppercase, and 2 special characters. To minimize brute force attacks, make sure the password does not contain words that can be found in the dictionary.*

Now retype the Password to confirm and press **DONE**

Whenever you log in to this **ROOT** user (*administrative*) account you will need to use this new password.

Don't forget it!

Creating User Accounts

Click on the **USER** Tab

Select **ADD USER**

User name:
Description:
Custom image:
Password:
Retype password:

Make sure the password you use is different from your ROOT account and, once again, has a minimum of 8 characters, with 2 uppercase, and 2 special characters.

Next, we will create file shares on the server. These can be left **Public** or made **Private** and/or **Secure** for added security.

Depending on the level of security your data requires, simply creating a single user account that has access to the files on Unraid Server might be enough security for your use case.

You can give full read/write access to the user or limit them to read-only on any of the shares created.

That being said. It's important to make a few shares Private to safeguard them from being accidentally erased or modified and even prevent them from being displayed to anyone accessing the server. We'll cover this in greater detail in the *Securing Your Unraid Server* section.

Setting Up Shares

Go to the **Shares Tab**

Click **Add Share** and call it Photos, Video, Docs, or anything you want

I'll create a **Photo** share for now and then a **Video** share. The method of organization is completely up to you. I'll show you my method in a minute.

Allocation method = High-water

This means the system will start filling up your first drive and once it arrives at 50% capacity it will then move to the second drive, fill it halfway, and once move to the next drive.

You can click on any option to see a drop-down window providing a description of its usage. We are going to create a basic setup so some of the options will not be addressed.

Setting Up Shares

Use cache disk = Yes

We set this to Yes so that all data goes to the cache disk before it is sent to the data storage drives. If set to No, all data going to your Unraid server will be written directly to the data storage drive which would be much slower.

SMB Security Settings

We want to leave these settings alone. By default, it will allow all computers on your local network to be able to interact with the files on your Unraid server.

Click Done

We will now see a Photo share that will be accessible through the entire network.

File Management

From the network/file browser (**PC**) or Finder (**MAC**), you should see the name of your new server. For me, it's **Harley** for you it's whatever you named the UnRaid server during installation.

If the user name you are using to access the Unraid server is the same, you will simply need to enter in your user password to gain access.

Here's an example of entering in Network Credentials to the Unraid Server called **Harley** using a user name of **joseph.** If there were additional users on this test machine they would be listed other user choices.

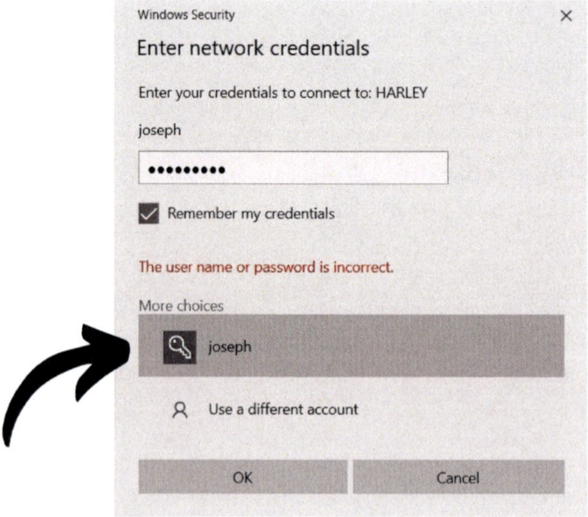

On the other hand, if the user you created on your Unraid server is different, you will need to click on *"Use a different account"* and enter in the username and password to gain access.

Transferring Files To Server

UnRaid Shares Are Available

You will now be able to see all of the shares that were automatically created by UnRaid as well as your **Photo** share.

Drag & Drop Files

At any point, you can drag and drop your files into the **Photo** folder from any directory/folder on your network.

Sub-Folder Organization

I like to create a sub-structure that helps keep my **client** and **personal** photos separate and organized.

"For every minute spent in organizing, an hour is earned"

- Benjamin Franklin

Sample Directory Structure

/Photos/**Clients**/Year/Month/Client_Name/Project_Name

.../Raw
.../Selected
.../Finals
.../PressReady

/Photos/**Personal**/Year/Month/Location/Name/

.../Raw
.../Selected
.../Finals
.../PrintReady

This directory structure allows me to sort through 100's of past clients, personal, and 1000's of projects to find a specific photo in minutes. You should come up with something that makes sense for your workflow.

Remember what Benjamin Franklin once said, "For every minute spent in organizing, an hour is earned."

"
Ransomware and other data theft threats are at an all-time high
"

How Much Security

Even though we are taking steps to secure your new Unraid server, bear in mind, even the “unpenetrable” Fort Knox, must continuously strengthen its security as technology becomes more and more advanced.

With today’s ransomware attacks and other exploits, we must do our part to mitigate access to our precious data. The following steps are a good starting point but are by no means an end all be all of the data security. There are entire books available dedicated solely to cyber-security. I would suggest you look to these documents for more advanced security measures, but keep in mind, even the strongest security in the world could be compromised by a single bad decision made while opening, reading, and clicking on a link or image within an email.

Now that the ROOT (admin) account is secured with a strong password we will create at least one additional account. You can create more accounts later based on the number of people requiring server access. This additional account will be used to access the UnRaid server and not the ROOT account. The ROOT account should only be used for administrative duties.

While this additional account can have the same username as the network computer accessing the Unraid Server, I would suggest both accounts have different passwords. Remember the SHARES we’re about to create will be available to everyone unless we specifically lock them down.

Security through obscurity should never be the only security mechanism but it is a good start!

The level of security should be directly proportional to the nature of the content secured and the environment where it will be stored.

Securing Your Unraid Server

Hiding System Shares

List of Shares that should be hidden from the network.

appdata
domains
isos
system
flash

All of the above shares besides the [**flash**] share can be modified within the **Share Tab**.

To change the [**flash**] share you will need to go into the **Main Tab**.

Select the **Share Tab**

Click on **appdata**

You will see a few different share options.

AFP Security Settings (*Apple Filing Protocol*)
Protocol for sharing with Apple devices

NFS Security Settings (*Network File System*)
Protocol for sharing with Linux devices

SMB Security Settings (*Server Message Block*)
Protocol for sharing with Windows devices

What does not need to be seen, shouldn't be
- Joseph Cristina

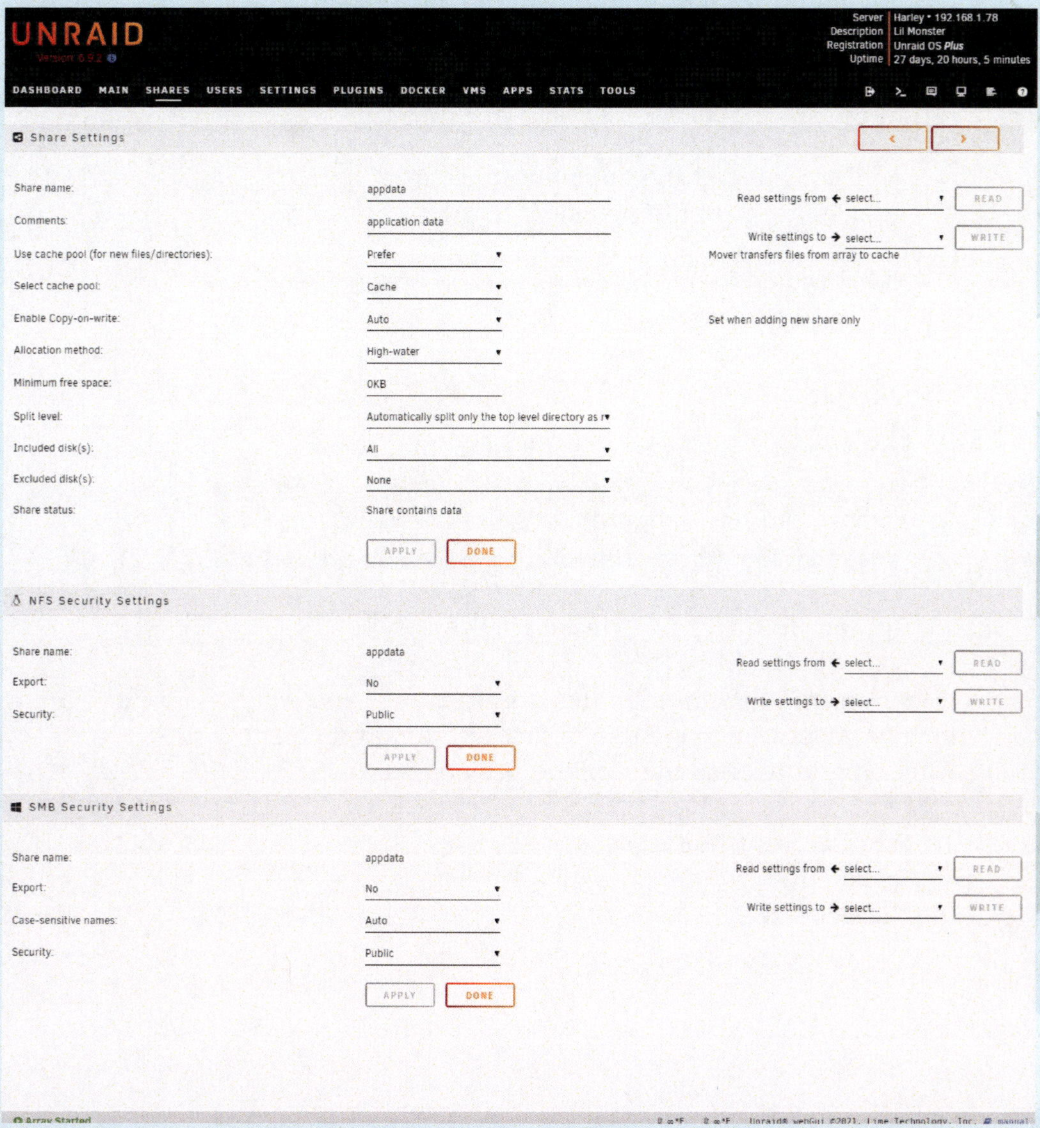
UNRAID
Server Harley • 192.168.1.78
Description Lil Monster
Registration Unraid OS Plus
Uptime 27 days, 20 hours, 5 minutes
DASHBOARD MAIN SHARES USERS SETTINGS PLUGINS DOCKER VMS APPS STATS TOOLS
Share Settings
Share name: appdata
Comments: application data
Use cache pool (for new files/directories): Prefer
Select cache pool: Cache
Enable Copy-on-write: Auto
Allocation method: High-water
Minimum free space: 0KB
Split level: Automatically split only the top level directory as r
Included disk(s): All
Excluded disk(s): None
Share status: Share contains data
Read settings from select... READ
Write settings to select... WRITE
Mover transfers files from array to cache
Set when adding new share only
APPLY DONE
NFS Security Settings
Share name: appdata
Export: No
Security: Public
Read settings from select... READ
Write settings to select... WRITE
APPLY DONE
SMB Security Settings
Share name: appdata
Export: No
Case-sensitive names: Auto
Security: Public
Read settings from select... READ
Write settings to select... WRITE
APPLY DONE
Array Started

Depending on what type of machine you will use to connect with the Unraid server, you will configure one or more of the above settings.

Change **Export** to “ **NO** “
This will stop the specific Share from being displayed on the network.

Alternatively, you can set **Export** to “ **YES** ” then click **Apply**

> Export allows the share to be seen on the network. The Security settings below allow you to specify not only who has access to the share but how much access they are granted.

Set the **Security to Private** click **Apply**

If you’ve created users on the Unraid server you will now be able to give access to any of them and select what type of access they will be provided.

Read/Write (Full Access **)**
Read Only
No Access

Select the **Main Tab**

Scroll down to **Boot Device**

Click on **Flash**

Follow the same procedure as above for either setting **Export** to

"**No**" so it will not be displayed at all

"**Yes**" if you would like the share to be accessed by a specific user.

> Be careful here... The Flash share is the Unraid Server's **Operating System**. Modifying this without a good understanding could render your UnRaid Server unusable or even worse, lead to data loss! You've been warned!

Removing Unneeded Services

Unless you need to access your Unraid Server via telnet I would suggest turning it off. You may also wish to turn off SSH but it does make troubleshooting a bit more difficult if you can't log in through a web browser.

Select the **Settings Tab**

Click on **Management Access**

Use TELNET: (set this to **NO**)

Click on **Apply**

Nine times out of ten you will directly access your data via your local network. In this case, you do not need an FTP server running on your Unraid so turn it off.

Select the **Settings Tab**

Click on **FTP Server**

Set FTP Server: (**Disabled**)

Click on **Apply** and **Done**

If there are any other services that you're 100% sure will not be needed, I would suggest turning them off.

Setting Up Alert Notifications

It is important to keep up to date with the health of your server. Keeping your Operating System, Plugins, and Dockers up to date is important to system security.

Select the **Settings Tab**

Click on **Notification Settings**

Set your **Unraid OS**, **Plugins**, and **Docker** notifications to **check one a day**

Under **Available Notifications**, by default, it's set to browser. This means that all notifications will be displayed on your Unraid Server Dashboard. You will need to log into your server daily to check for critical updates, array status, notices, warnings, and alerts.

This is fine to start but I would suggest adding Email or one of the other numerous methods to deliver notifications to your computer, phone, or other platforms that you may frequent: example Discord

Take time to figure out which notification method works the best for providing you with the most stress-free server administration.

"It's not if but when you'll be hit with a power failure"
BE PREPARED

Uninterrupted Power Supplies (UPS)

Safeguarding against data loss and/or corruption

Before completing this basic setup, we want to plug the server into and configure a UPS backup power unit. In case of a power failure, the Unraid Server would be less likely to experience any data loss or corruption.

Even if the server doesn't experience data loss or corruption due to a power failure, the system would still require a full parity check which could take many hours or even days depending on the size of your array to complete. A UPS prevents this scenario.

I recommend an APC brand UPS battery backup unit as they are generally compatible right out of the box and require very little time to configure. Read "Safe Power-Cycling" below before installing the UPS battery backup.

1VA = 1Watt of DC power. The amount of time before the backup battery runs out of power depends on how much load is placed on the UPS and at times the quality of the unit itself.

Purchase a UPS with a VA rating twice the maximum amount of watts your system could use but keep in mind not all UPS are created equal. Purchase a name-brand quality unit over a cheaper one.

Example: 750W max load system could be best paired with a 1500VA UPS.

Review the **My Parts List / Power Supply** section for assistance in purchasing the UPS.

Safe Power-Cycling

How-to safely power-cycle your server

Bear in mind before installing a UPS or powering down your server, it's important to follow the steps below.

If the server shuts down due to power failure or improper power-cycling there could be data loss or corruption or at least the system will require a full parity check of all attached storage which could take many hours or even days depending on the size of your array to complete. Before installing a UPS follow the power-cycling steps below to prevent this scenario.

Proper Shut-Down

From The **MAIN** menu tab under **Array Operation**

Click **STOP**
The Stop will take the array off-line.

Once the array is STOPPED click **SHUTDOWN**
The Shutdown will activate a clean system power down.

Proper Power On

From The **MAIN** menu tab under **Array Operation**

Click **START**
The start will take the array online.

Once the array is started you will be able to access all of the data on the server.

UPS Battery Backup Configuration

Once your server is properly powered down, plug the server's power cord into the battery backup, connect a USB cable from the UPS battery backup to the server, and reboot.

Now you may bring your array back online as described in ***Starting The Array.***

UPS Configuration

Got to the **SETTINGS** menu tab

System Settings

Click **UPS Settings**

The standard setup is just about perfect.

Set **Start APC UPS daemon** is set to **YES**

Set **UPS cable** and **UPS type** is set to **USB**

The rest of the setting is a personal preference.

From the Unraid **DASHBOARD** check the **POWER** section. UPS Load: should remain under 80% utilization. If you see it spike higher under load a larger capacity UPS would be advised.

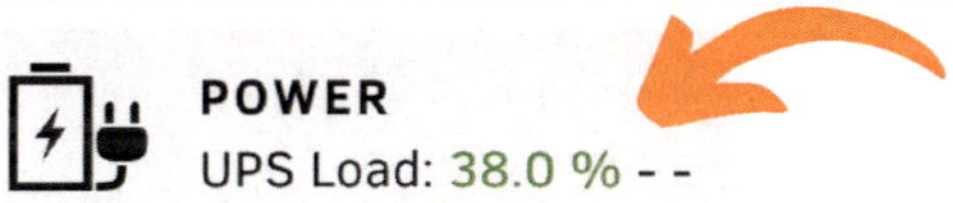

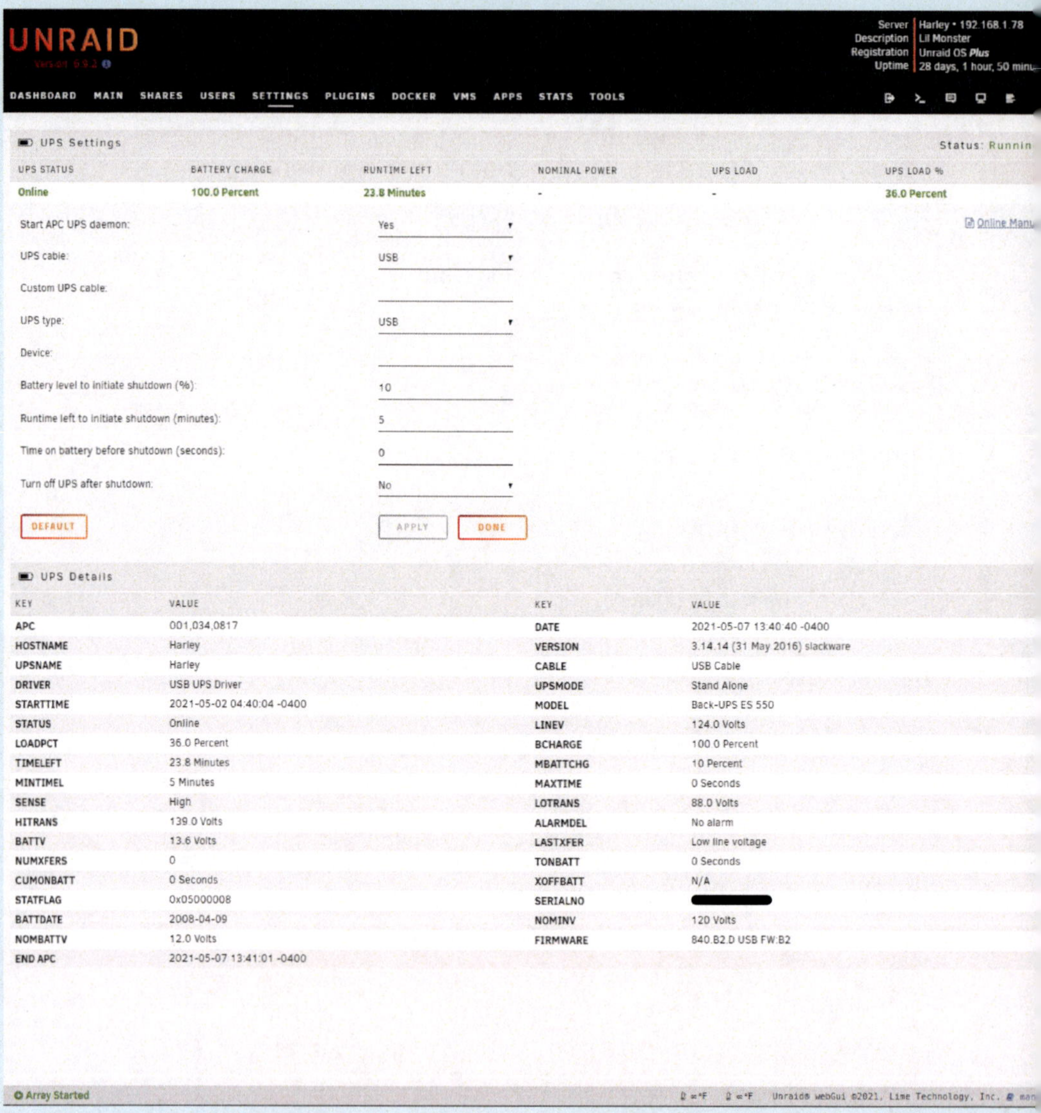
UNRAID
Server Harley • 192.168.1.78
Description Lil Monster
Registration Unraid OS Plus
Uptime 28 days, 1 hour, 50 minu
DASHBOARD MAIN SHARES USERS SETTINGS PLUGINS DOCKER VMS APPS STATS TOOLS
UPS Settings
Status: Runnin
UPS STATUS BATTERY CHARGE RUNTIME LEFT NOMINAL POWER UPS LOAD UPS LOAD %
Online 100.0 Percent 23.8 Minutes - - 36.0 Percent
Online Manu
Start APC UPS daemon: Yes
UPS cable: USB
Custom UPS cable:
UPS type: USB
Device:
Battery level to initiate shutdown (%): 10
Runtime left to initiate shutdown (minutes): 5
Time on battery before shutdown (seconds): 0
Turn off UPS after shutdown: No
DEFAULT
APPLY
DONE
UPS Details
KEY VALUE KEY VALUE
APC 001,034,0817
HOSTNAME Harley
UPSNAME Harley
DRIVER USB UPS Driver
STARTTIME 2021-05-02 04:40:04 -0400
STATUS Online
LOADPCT 36.0 Percent
TIMELEFT 23.8 Minutes
MINTIMEL 5 Minutes
SENSE High
HITRANS 139.0 Volts
BATTV 13.6 Volts
NUMXFERS 0
CUMONBATT 0 Seconds
STATFLAG 0x05000008
BATTDATE 2008-04-09
NOMBATTV 12.0 Volts
END APC 2021-05-07 13:41:01 -0400
DATE 2021-05-07 13:40:40 -0400
VERSION 3.14.14 (31 May 2016) slackware
CABLE USB Cable
UPSMODE Stand Alone
MODEL Back-UPS ES 550
LINEV 124.0 Volts
BCHARGE 100.0 Percent
MBATTCHG 10 Percent
MAXTIME 0 Seconds
LOTRANS 88.0 Volts
ALARMDEL No alarm
LASTXFER Low line voltage
TONBATT 0 Seconds
XOFFBATT N/A
SERIALNO [redacted]
NOMINV 120 Volts
FIRMWARE 840.B2.D USB FW:B2
Array Started
Unraid® webGui ©2021, Lime Technology, Inc.

Adding APPS To Unraid

Community Apps Plugin

Optional but recommended as it provides an easy way of adding countless useful apps to your server.

The URL provided below may change over time, you may wish to open a web browser and Google Search for Unraid *community apps plugin*

https://unraid.net/community/apps

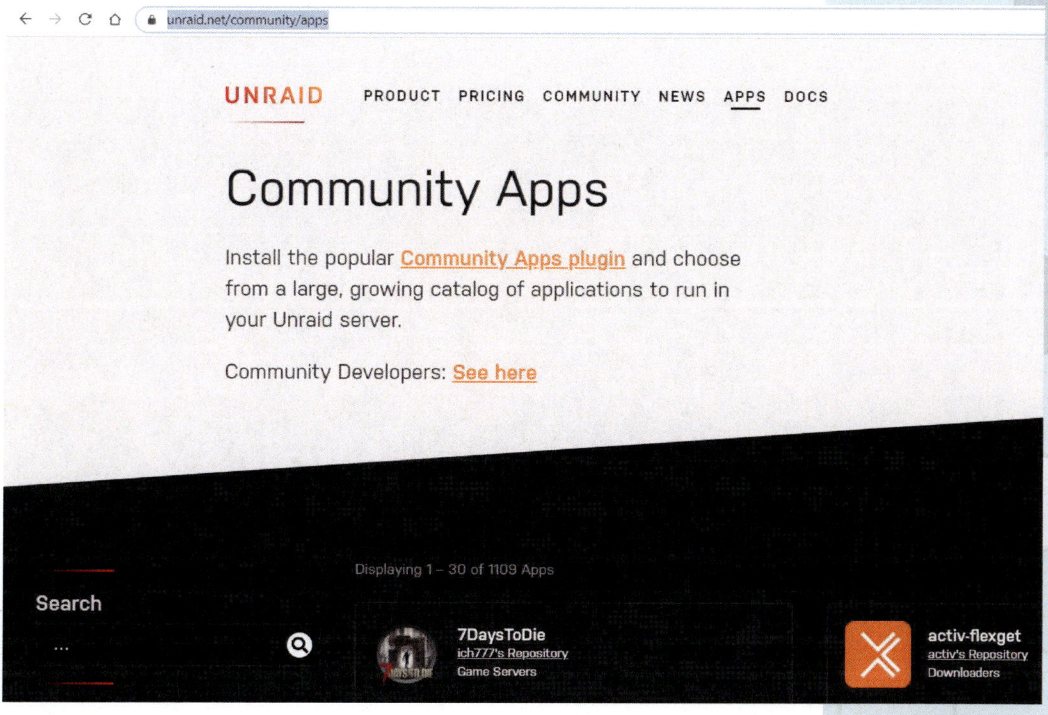

Where To Get Apps TAB Plugin

Click On the **Community Apps plugin**

If the page has not moved you should end up here, if not remember to use Google Search.

https://forums.unraid.net/topic/38582-plug-in-community-applications/

Scroll down until you see **INSTALLATION**

To install this plugin, paste the following URL into the Plugins / Install Plugin section:

Copy the **URL** provided

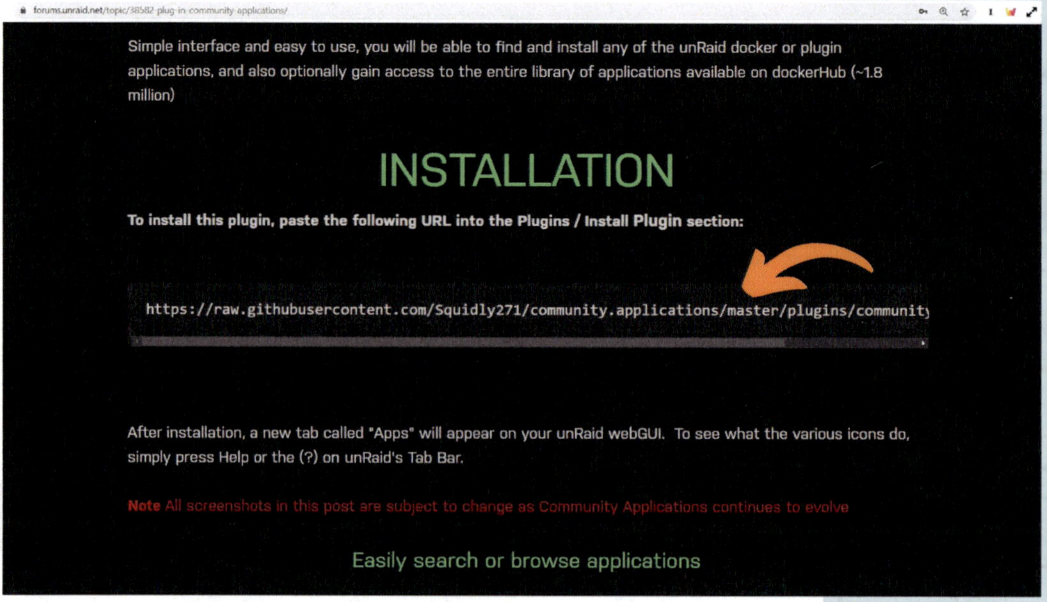

APPS Tab Installation

From the Unraid control panel select the **PLUGINS** Tab

Select **Install Plugin**

Paste The **URL** you copied into the field provided:

Enter URL of remote plugin file or local plugin file

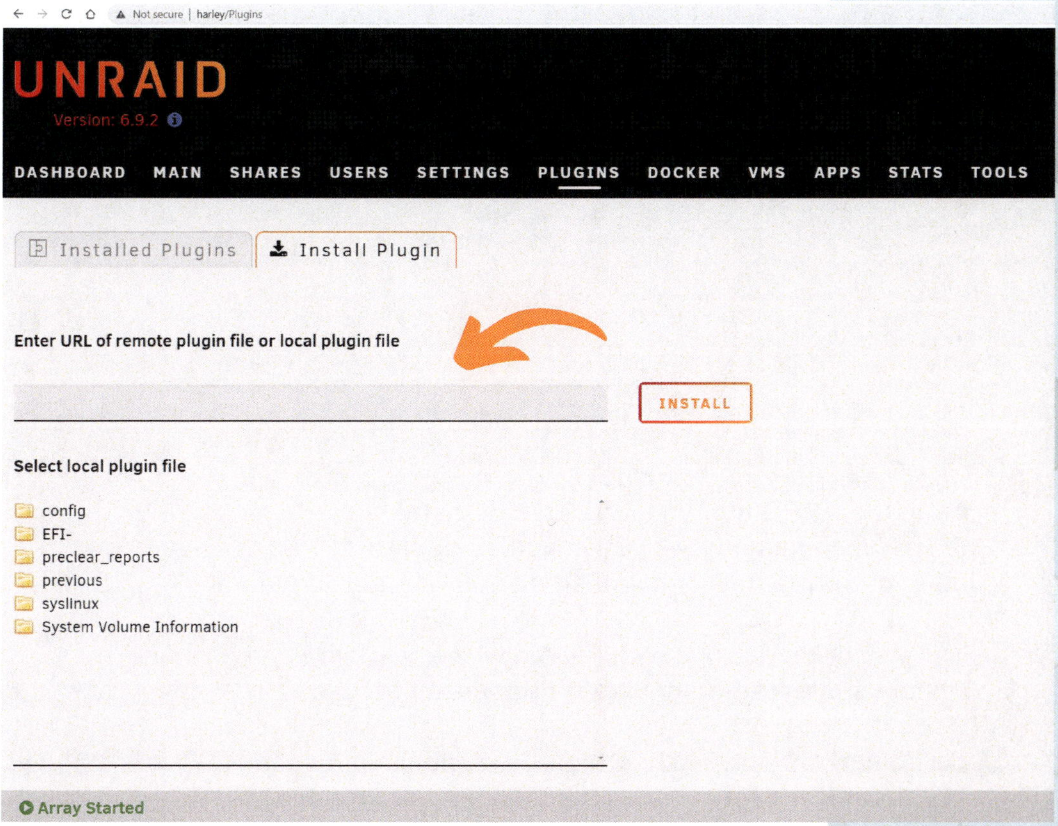

APPS Tab Use Case

You should now see a new TAB available called **APPS**. If not, you may need to refresh your web browser so your Unraid Server control panel refreshes.

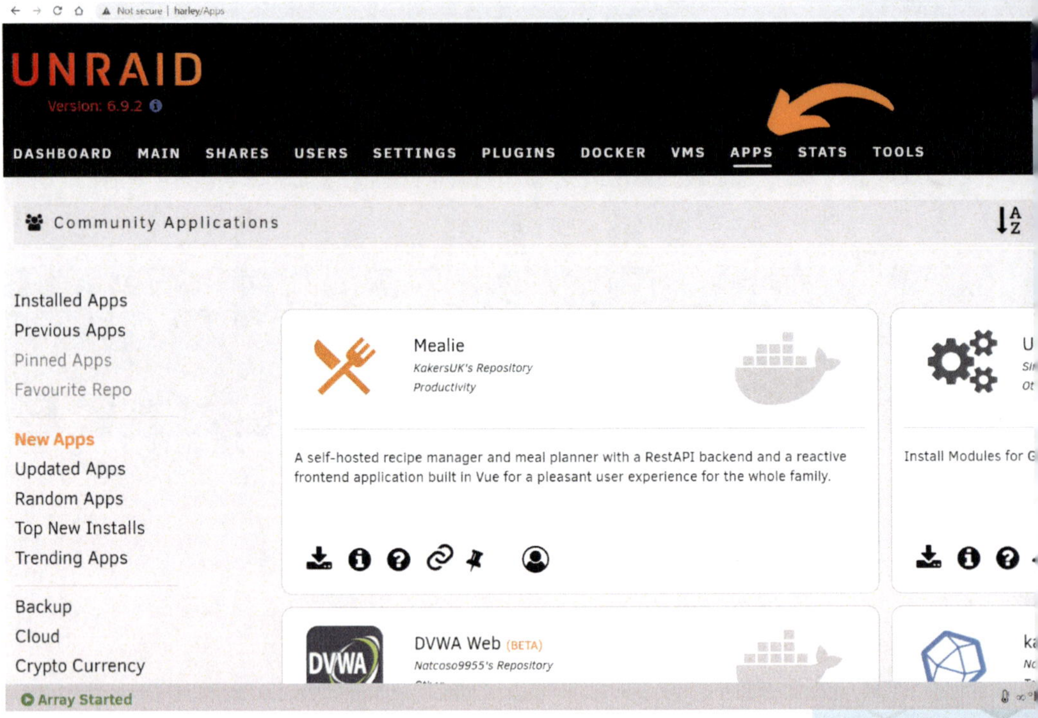

From the APPS tab, you'll be able to install a plethora of useful community APPS as well as update APPS that you've previously installed on your Unraid Server.

The use of these APPS will have to be a book in itself. If there's interest I may take on the task.

Until then you may wish to install an application called **Fix Common Problems** as it's designed to find and suggest solutions to common configuration problems.

Unraid USB Backup

Once you've configured your Unraid server to your liking, this might take a few days or even weeks, but I would highly recommend backing up the USB Key that holds your Operating System and all of its settings.

From The **MAIN** menu tab under Boot Device

Click **Flash**

Under **Flash Device Settings**

Click **Flash Backup**

You will see:

Please wait... creating Flash backup zip file (this may take several minutes)

A ZIP file called [ServerName]-flash-backup-[date]-xxxx will be created and downloaded to your computer.

This file is an archive of your entire boot drive including the operating system and all of your settings.

Store this somewhere for safekeeping. If your USB Key was to fail you should be able to get up and running within minutes without the need to reconfigure all of your Unraid Server settings.

Auto vs Manual Backup

Backup strategies are different for everyone based on the level of security required and the amount of data that changes over the course of time.

One strategy would be to purchase backup software for your specific operating system that would allow for scheduling, minutely, hourly, and/or daily backups. This software will not be discussed in this publication but maybe in future writes.

Another strategy would be to manually backup files and/or directories of changed data. This means if you were to say work on a client project or maybe edit from photos when you're done you would simply drag the folder or its contents into a folder on the Unraid server but if you are one to forget to drag and drop changed files as needed, the automatic backup strategy would be better for your use case.

Be careful with automatic backups as being able to set it and forget it very appealing and does provide safety even when you forget the problem is if you were hit with a virus, trojan, ransomware attack, or even were to delete a file or folder and not recognize issue before the automatic backup runs, you could copy over good file with corrupt or delete files unknowingly.

There is no perfect system and the auto vs manual backup strategy should be carefully thought through by you as you analyze your personal use case.

Author's Biography

Joseph began studying in the visual arts at the age of eight under his mentor, Marsha Nardini, an incredible commercial mural painter and installation artist with studios in New York City. She passed along practical, creative and intuitive knowledge that greatly influenced his entire career. His reverence continues many years after her passing.

He was formally educated at Florida Atlantic University and the Art Institute of Fort Lauderdale in the early '90s with degrees in commercial photo/video production, computer science, and child psychology. His first employment was with an advertising agency doing magazine paste-up, layout, and cover work.

His career path deviated from the arts to the computer industry when the opportunity arose to start his own software business. While lucrative, this move stifled his creativity and motivated him, after 13 years, to sell the business and move back into arts as a multimedia studio owner, Allure Multimedia, LLC.

He's educated tens of thousands of fellow photographers worldwide as the co-host of the popular podcast Digital Photography Cafe, with weekly discussions focusing on the art, business, and current trends in the world of visual media. After 8 years, Joseph started his own Youtube channel and continues to provide what he calls edutainment each week.

As a photographer and videographer for over 20 years, Joseph found many products he used deficient. With this in mind, he began inventing products for himself and once perfected, offered them to other photographers and videographers under the brand JCristina, LLC.

Joseph is the inventor of the patent-pending Focus Pyramid, an auto-focus lens calibration tool used by thousands of photo and video professionals and schools around the world. The PRT – Photo Reference Tool with its Dual-Axis Color Control used to dial in White Balance at the time of capture or in post-production and has recently launched Aurora Camera Care a division of JCristina, LLC specializing in the care of camera sensors, lenses, and more.

From his roots in fine art, design, and computer science to his many years of photo/video experience, today Joseph is an author, inventor, educator, and freelance director of photography who continues to give back to the creative community by authoring educational books and producing free YouTube content consisting of industry news, reviews, howtos, and commentary.

Joseph's day-to-day collaborations produce content that moves and inspires, while his many products help fellow creatives become more productive.

Additional Information & Resources

For more information consult the Unraid WIKI

https://wiki.unraid.net

Cooler Master Power Supply Calculator

https://www.coolermaster.com/power-supply-calculator/

I've curated a list of Unraid Server hardware part ideas that may help with your selection.

https://jcristina.com/unraid

Visit my Youtube channel for the latest photo, video, and tech news, reviews, howtos, and commentary.

https://youtube.com/jcristina

Additional books can be found here.

https://jcristina.com/books

Join our creative community on our Discord Server.

https://community.jcristina.com

Need to clean your camera sensor? Calibrate your DSLR camera's autofocus system? Maybe dial in your photo/video color? Well, I got you covered! Find these and many products I've invented on my website.

https://jcristina.com

Glossary

AFP - AppleTalk Filing Protocol is a Mac OS file protocol that allows users to access files between devices.

FTP - File Transfer Protocol allows for the transfer of files between a server and a client on a computer network.

GUID - Globally Unique IDentifier is a 128-bit number that is used to identify user accounts, documents, software, hardware, software interfaces, sessions, database keys, and other items.

NFS - Network File System is a protocol that allows a user on a client computer to access files over a network.

RAID - Redundant Array of Independent Disks

Server - A computer or program which manages access to a centralized resource or service in a network.

SMB - is a protocol that creates a connection between the server and the client by sending multiple request-response messages between the devices.

Telnet - Telnet is an application protocol to provide tex communication using a virtual terminal connection.

USB Key - also known as a USB Stick or USB Drive, is a flash drive or small device for storing and moving data.

UPS - Uninterrupted Power Supply (battery backup), provides backup power when your regular power source fails or voltage drops to an unacceptable level.

FREE GIFT

10 Tips For Creating Tack Sharp Photos

A photographer's guide to sharper images

jcristina.com/10tips

As a thank you for your purchase, please enjoy this eBook at no charge!

@JosephCristina @JosephCristina JCristina JCristina.com

Made in United States
Orlando, FL
04 November 2026

90201658R00059